The Rob Dog Story

Narrated by Mum

Margaret Anderson

Published by New Generation Publishing in 2020

First Edition

ISBN 978-1-80031-537-2

www.newgeneration-publishing.com

New Generation Publishing

My Pack

Early Memories

I have only a few memories of my earliest years. There was a tiny human who interested me. I can still recall her cooing noises and pleasant dampy smell in the box on wheels. I was proud of this bundle but not allowed too near. During these early years I learnt to change a nappy, and duck when a full black bag came flying toward me.

When I was 2 ½ Springs, I Was taken to a compound full of my own Kind. Dogs in one area and bitches next door. I ran and barked and loved this company, but there was competition here as every dog was looking for their own human pack. It was here that I chose my lifetime Mistress and her clan. My Pack consisted of Dad, Mum, Brother Rich, Sister Cath and Mistress Mary.

They came for me and I recognised them immediately.

The Pad

We drove home in the car. At home I was introduced to Dad. He told me that he provided the tins. On this occasion there was a welcome bowl full of meaties and always after this my provider, provided. I didn't forget to return to the hand that cut up this food, to thank mistress and daub a little scent of this delicious repast wiping my whiskers on her lap. I explored 'The Pad' which proved satisfactory. I had a good stretch of running grass, and it took me some days to mark this area.

Gradually I learnt the communication words of my pack. Food is "Meaties", but first food of the day "Breck Lets" 'Stay in them gardens' meaning we are not going out. ''Walkies'' plus the lead never failed to get me barking in excitement.

From day one I got the walking clock routine. Mary understood that I had to walk outside ''them gardens" morning and evening. There are open meadows to gallop across, and I liked to run like the wind. In straight lines after a scent, or in circles round and round in joy. Because, as Dad said "I had landed on my paws." I often ran and barked in delight.

Between the beds

My Barstick

There was a hitch in this arrival. It was intended that I should sleep downstairs in the laundry room, that is where my barstick was put. At night the door was shut. Don't get me wrong, I liked the smell of our laundry, especially before it was put into the round and round window, but not alone at night. I scratched and cried. It was Mum or Dad who came down and up stairs over a series of nights. First my barstick was brought into the eating room, but even here it was lonely, especialling on moonshine nights. So I howled. Eventually I was allowed upstairs into my proper night accommodation on a rug between the beds of my Mistress Mary and Sister Cath.

Once I had taken charge I could guard the house from every room. I would bark, a friendly one, to all approaching humans, then the pack would decide if they wished the caller to enter or not.

We never had the burglars.

My barstick remained in the eating room and contained my sheepskin rug. When the house became over crowded with human feet, I found this refuge.

Some times Mistress would tell me off, saying "In your barstick" with that pointing finger. I would crawl with bended knees into my comfortable den and look up at her with on so sad eyes.

Meaties and Mince Pies

My stomach clock would sound at 6pm. Then I would use the eye catching signal to indicate to Mistress Mary that now was the moment to get out the tin opener and measure half-a-pound-of meaties. As this often co-incided with the evening run, I could give the sharp bark signal and stand posed in the kitchen door, with that hungry eye message.

Brecklets was All-in-one dog food. Ruff Stuff. Dad had a few bowls of this, by mistake, and said he 'prefurred' cereals. We were in agreement here. I really did 'prefurr' human food whenever available.

Human fodder came in two ways. While walking out near our Pub sometimes I would catch the whiff of discarded grub under the hedge. One quick dive under the branches and it was mine.

The second method was from the plates.

'Oh no, I never begged!'

As the pack ate their meal, I would sit silently near bye, keeping the ear on the movements and waiting for that sound of collecting up the plates. Then you make yourself seen, catch the eye, and move the look toward the scraps on the plates. These scraps would then be 'transfurred' to my bowl.

I was unable to resist pastry. One day some warm mince pies, mouth drooling, were left unattended on the table. I could not help myself. One by one I took them to eat on the door mat. Leaving no crumbs. I had to chuckle inside as Mum tried to fathom out where they had disappeared.

Fun and Games

My secondary education took place at The Dog Training class. I was instructed in the art of sit, heel, and stay. I became competent in all these positions, but I put my paw down when I was expected to retrieve an old pair of Dad's socks.

A Collie is not a Retriever!

We had fun 'in them garden'. I liked to play the catch ball game. I would run from one catcher to another until someone missed. Then I would leap into the air and catch up the 'ballie.' It took some persuasion to get me 'to leave' this lovely chew. Another game I loved involved a piece of tough blue plastic tubing. I sank my teeth into one end while Rich held the other swinging me off my paws and in circles in the air.

Then there was the rattle the door knob game, shouting squirrels. These little grey animals ran along the grass under the walnut trees. I loved to rush out shrieking and chase them across the ground. I never caught one and was often left "Barking up the wrong tree."

The Warren and The Water

In my youth I could out run a rabbit. On good days a rabbit chase could take me out of ear shot.   Mary would call 'Robbie over and over but when one is on the 'deep scent' the ears get blocked. In our backfield there was a warren. I have spent some wonderful hours sniffing into bolt holes and digging with all four paws. I am a slim dog and could fit into little holes. Unfortunately, being long haired, the dusty mud would cling to the fur. So on return from these happy episodes it was usually bath night.

The thing I could never abide was "Water on the Fur!" I remember when I had not seen large water. I was running along our path by the bank, I saw green weeds and green reflexion, so I jumped, as I always do on an edge. Then I felt terrible cold wet and I was under the stuff. A shock for a dog.

My pack on the bank pulled me out with human grins on their faces.

I hope that I gave them a good shaking shower.

Communication

Talking of "Walkies" and I love to talk about walkies. My favourite place was The Town Park. Here we had a circle to complete, following in the wake of many exotic dog scents. This place is paradise to the nose, and a meeting place for the canine populous of Bedford. If we drove along Park Avenue, I would indicate for the driver to stop by sitting bolt upright on the black seat, and stare fixedly in the park direction. This seemed to impress my pack who seemed surprised that I could sniff out the Park Stop.

Humans have no idea of the scent pictures we dogs see. A dog will know what is for supper or who you have been patting, simply by smelling your hands and clothes.

The best scent pictures come from people like our friendly Postie. I could see all the dogs she visited on her daily round when she allowed me to take a long clothes sniff. If I were a person I'd be a Postie when I grew up.

I scented communications every day in Shambrook. On each 'walkie' a dog would know who was out and about. The pack rely on different communications. They can only recognise a few doggy phrases and some body poses. I will write down a few.

High pitched excited bark = Isn't it about time

With a lot of running about + I am coming too.

One quick yap = time to get on

Short sharp barks = Please open the door

The yelp = that hurt

The growly bark = Grumble weeds

Snarl with curled lip = Get off

Loud regular lots of noise = Someone approaching

The shriekie joy with tail and body twists = I am so glad you are home.

Gradually my pack got the messages but dogs often need to persist as humans do get blocked cars.

Happy Days

When my young pack were learning at that place called school, my walks were fitted in quickly before and after. Holidays were best. First was the 'lye in'. You might get mistress up with a wet nose in the face and a few loud yaps in the ear, but patience was needed. Once the pack were out of bed our day was tied together. Long walkies and extra pieces off the plates, coupled with personal talks and all day pats.

While mistress watches the moving box you snuggle up, use your nose to lift the hand and sit while she tickles the ears and smooths the coat. Or you can lye on the back for a relaxed tummy rub by the fire side. Blissful.

I am a most handsome chap to look on, with my soft Black Coat and brown and white highlights. I looked my best after a grooming, another pleasant occupation as long as no one thought about water. One small problem could be mud which would collect between the claws. I could dispose of this with the teeth grooming process depositing it on the 'carpit,'but mistress insisted on 'washing them feeties' wet again!

Vets and Visits

When thinking of grooming. I recall that I was entered into a dog show where I won First Prize- one dog chew I believe I received, for being the best Cross Collie. Mistress Mary was presented with a shiney cup and red ribbon.

I was so cross (Collie) Ha Ha, and as I paraded in the next class for ''The dog the Vet would like to take home" I snarled at the dog behind me. Well, who wanted to go home with the Vet?

In fact I liked my visits to the vet. He had a good smelling premises and his white coat usually had the right perfumes. Once each year I was lifted onto his table for something called a 'Prick' I was always engrossed in the fuss and did not get to understand what this Prick was all about.

The Prick however was a prelude to my own holiday. My mistress would look sad as she collected my barstick and lead. Off we drove to my holiday camp. Here were all kinds of joyful barking friends. We would chorus together late into many nights until some of us lost our bark boxes.

In this camp our individual Kennels had on-suite outside runs. One night I decided to make a break out. I jumped and jumped until I had made a gap in the wire roof wide enough for me to squeeze through. Out I went and had a night on the chicken wire roof. I communed with the bitches and chatted with the dogs. I was just exploring the surrounding field, chasing the odd rabbit, when I was spied and collected in.

Sadly I lost the on-suite run, but it had been a night to remember.

The Grands in Devon

I loved to be "Going in the car" once there, I had the most happy knowledge that my pack was complete and where we went we went together. Sometimes it was the rough and tumble of us on the back seat. If it was a longtime sat by Mums feet in the front well, and the big clothes boxes were packed into the car boot. These journeys took us to the Grands in Devon.

Here was the great salt water. My pack liked to immurse themselves in this wet. I had to bark shout to them from the shore and avoid those moving wet wavey edges. I was glad the Grands didn't go in the wet. Grandad liked to walk me when the pack wasn't about. I was the Grands favourite Grandog, but I was not destined to be an Old Sea Dog.

I recall going onto the beach and finding that the only leg cocking upright was one deck chair a good run away. Off I shot to this convenience. It supported a persons jacket and smelt fine. At that moment there was "A shout about my ears and stones beneath my feet."

This I didn't expect.

A short car ride from the Grands is The Moors. I know why it is called moor, because there is more of this than one can cover in a days walking. We have walked all day across terrain and seen so much moor. Wonderful days climbing to high places and stopping to sniff out the animal tracks while the pack sit and view the views. Then running down to the valley and the little streams you could drink if you were thirsty.

We had spent hundreds of hols: at the Grands and I knew the area like the back of my paw.

Absailing

When I was young, or was it when I could hear, I detested those Buzz flyers. I snapped at them and one day caught one in the mouth. Such a stab! After this, if I heard the dreaded Buzzzz I would run, even out of the window if that was the only way out. Once my Cath caught me by the back legs as I dangled from her window.

When my pack said "Got to wait." I knew what was expected. In winter I might retire upstairs and relax on mistress's bed. I had to be ready to make a quick fly off, attempting to kick the blankets straight behind me, as I heard approaching voices. Summer time could be agony when evading perfume wafted in through the window. One day, this became too much to bear, and I found I could abscol down from the back window using the virginia creeper. While it was believed that I was shut indoors, I enjoyed a full days outing. A visit to my best bitch Gem, and then a Grand Tour of the village.

I frequently managed a breakaway. Either I would quietly sneak out of the gate or disappear following the blocked ear chase. If I got caught sneaking off I was "Nicked," Gem lived in her outdoor Kennel in the valley air stream only 5 minutes along the Paw Path. She and her pal cider were always pleased to see me. Gem is a pretty cross like me and Cider he golden play fellow. I know Gem's mistress well, but I never let her catch my collar.

I always came home from these outings, but the pack had to worry. I do understand they troubled that I might arrive in the road at the same time as a "Brum brum." They forgot that I had been taught to sit at the side of the road, look and listen. If I should get lost, I never did, I wore my collar with my name a talking machine number on my tinkling disc.

The only time I let people read my dis was when I was some miles away with my stomach clock at meatie time. Mum would arrive to give me a lift home in the car. She would say "Naughty Boy" It was the way she said Naughty that made you feel bad, but when the scent calls a Dodge has to try to dodge out.

Gentle Patting Aunty

We frequently drove to Walthamstow to visit our gentle 'Aunty Gladioli.' She liked me and put down a bowl of milkies for my arrival. Once I travelled with her on an underground train. I can recall the awful noise the carriage made as it passed under the earth. All I could do was jump on top of her suitcase and bury my popping ears next to my Mistress. Next we get Aunty onto another train for Devon. Mum get on to settled her in. This train began to move off with me and my young mistress standing on the platform. We all shouted, and mum jumped off just in time.

We had a holiday near Aunty's Pad. Living under a canvas roof in the Big Forest. Every day we walked among the trees. It was here I saw a snake curled up sleeping in the sunshine. It hissed at us, and I was strickly told not to sniff at this creature. Since then I have noticed families of these creatures in our back field, little thready baby wiggles darting through the grass and not to be sniffed at. Under canvas each night we cooked sausages or best stake on bonfire, we all smelt off bonfire and outdoors. As there was no bathroom here, my packs scent was worth a good sniff.

Gentle patting Aunty come to live at the Gentle Old Folkes Home in Shambrook. As you know my coat is soft, and as a regular visitor, I found plenty of gentle patting clients. I have to admit that I am not as patient as the Pat Dogs. When I was ready to leave for the walk home, I would give the Loud Yap. This would make everyone jump and hurry my mistress to say the goodbyes.

Pets

There were other live in pets at our Pad. Hammy the Hampster who darted about our bedroom leaving a rodent scent. I had something in common with Ham. He was an absailor from the upper window and he got 'Nicked' among garden flowers. After him came the long haired Ham who was brought up as a student nurse and knew a lot about pricks.

We had 3 'Fadits' short for 'You have had it' unlike the wild rabbits, these had a tinge of pack scent, and were not chaseable. Sadly they got something called 'mixi' which makes rabbit poorly. My Cath nursed them with great care, but they didn't recover. Sometimes wild Rabbit get mixi. My Mum would call me out to dispatch these poor fadits because I finished them off neatly.

Our other live in was Emma the horse, she lived in the stable or out on the field. Mum and I went daily to the field. Northfork, where I sniffed out all the animal scents living in our barn. I would call my hunting Yap Yap so Mum would know all was well underneath the hay stack. Families of rabbit, mice, rats and a stoat family lived here. Foxes came hunting for meaties for their cubs. Dear deer occasionally chased over, and flocks of birds rested on the field. A large cat with no tail lived in our barn and sometimes left rabbit meaties behind for me on his straw table.

Occasionally Mum would ride out on a quiet Sunday morning and I ran beside Em. I soon learnt to run ahead on the green swards so that I wasn't left behind on the gallop stretches.

Suize, The Black Vietnamese Pot Belly Pig, was a regular visitor to the field. Her smell was wonderful, when we romped her aroma rubbed off on my fur. When I returned home there were such crys of "Ugh" and the wet buckets came out.

For a short time 3 Baa's came to stay while they were on the bottle. Everyone said that I might have made a good sheep dog, but by the time rams were half grown they could bole me over. They were the pet sort, and ran towards you, while most sheep run away. The rams returned to the farm, but Primpose the ewe stayed with us and now lives with her friend on the field.

Neighbours

Next door lived Little short legged Bella, she had a pointed nose like mine. Behind the long fence lived large curly Hagges both these neighbours had happy friendly ways. But Jumble and Buster encroached onto my territory. At the first moment I knew that these two male dogs were not to be trusted.   We had same wonderful punch ups. I could snarl and flash my teeth against the Bullish noses. Tough Guys.

When Bella and Hagges departed this life their pads were run by Young Monty the Dash, and Seggah the curly. Seggah is Haggis backwards, although she always went forward. Both these friends were comfortable to scent about. Monty Sometimes popped in and had a look into my bowl, as I never left anything worthwhile in my bowl, this was quite ok.

Receintly a number of moggies have moved into the neighbourhood. As far as a dog is concerned these cats tend to "sit on the fence". The night air sometimes rings with loud Meeows of the feline squabbles, probably fighting over a mousie morsel.

Cats can be clever hunters. Osca will pass bye with a mouthful of mouse for his bowlie, Little Tiga sits by the buddleia catching butterflies, while Caspa stays to watch over his pad and waits for his human to fill his bowlie from the tins.

I have to smile inside at young Mango when he attempted to look Tigarish. Hair standing on end in a pouncing pose and showing his little teeth. I would wander by indicating that I had not noticed him.

The Seasons

The quantum theory of Dogs - walking places vary according to the time available to the mistress.

A shot one - around my back field.

A medium one - to the Felmersham Reserve.

A long one - over the fields and far aways.

I recall these places in all the seasons.

WINTER walks in crisp white snow. I ran in circles in this exciting coolness and rolled over and over in the lovely softness. First thing in the morning my paw prints were the first to mark this virgin surface. Humans can see and follow rabbit, fox, or deer tracks, but I scented the animal in each foot print, their odour individual and piquant in this icy air.

SPRING and a freshness of plants growing green with gentle fragrance of the sap rising. We had to keep off the little shoots of crops and walk again around the edge of the fields. As the hours of light increase and the sad began to warm, my coat began to molt leaving hair on "the carpit." Fur useful for lining nests, and young animals were being born all about us. There were youngsters a plenty in our barn.

SUMMER Sunny days dabbling in the river. I recall following my young pack as they climbed the bending Willow tree over the deep water River. We looked down into running water for tiddlers and frogs. Although my people jumped into the wet, I was careful to climb down backwards to keep my fur dry this time.

The Summer grasses would grow taller than me. As I ran through the fields would leap above the growth to spy my mistress and show her my position every few minuits. The dry ripe aroma filled the nostrils, as the time approached for cutting the grasses. This fodder, for the cloven hoof, was stacked in lumps. Mum collected her lumps in the car, bouncing about our field I liked to sit ontop of the load of bales as they were brought down to the barn, but I was reproached as I went to mark them for us.

AUTUMN brought out the macks and wellies.

Out in the morning damp, when the sky was full of yellow, brown leaves, I would catch a tinge of the damp coat of a visiting fox, deer, or badger. Our compost heap warm and 'nurey' invited other visitors looking for their winter dens and leaving their calling cards and scenty trails Mole, Hedge Hog, and field mice kept me searching the garden.

Autumn also heralded the problems of wet on the fur and mud between the claws. I needed a lot of Rubber Dubs' with my towel during this time of year. To compensate, a dog could dry off best by the nice warm fire.

Good days, bad days.

Everyone in my pack learnt to drive the car. I have sat on the back seat observing their progress. In turn Richard, Mary and Catherine have frog -hopped and bumped around the field. Mum instructed in a calm strained voice, while she held tightly to both sides of the front seat and put her right foot down hard on the car floor.

Eventually Mum Looked relaxed, lessons were taken, and the **L** disappeared. Then we could all go anywhere.

But there was one day we were out in the car and the pack carefully studied a large ordinance survey map. We stopped at a good walking place, but they left me behind shut in the car! I looked at this map left beside me on the seat. I could see hills and dales and running places, and I became a very cross Collie. To convey my deep displeasure, I sank my teeth into the map and with my paw I tore across the paper showing this lovely walking country. When they saw this, my pack felt bad and the tom map was kept in the car as a reminder that   A dog got to go

I liked to sit on the front seat beside my young folk, watching the road coming toward me and enjoying the speed. I became expert at "Road surfing" around the bends of the country Lanes.

Mary and Cath often drove to our favourite place Harrold Country Park. Here we promenaded around the Lake, meeting other walkers and scenting wild creatures. Sometimes this walk ended up in 'The Pub'. Great, when the weather was dry and we sat outside on or under the picnic tables. Crisps and cheesie delicacies known as 'Little Cheesies' from the plough mans plate would slip under the table. Not so good on wet days when I "Go to stay" in the car. However The Pub Place pleased my people and they came out smiling and allowed me to rub my wet fur against them as we drove home.

Christmas

I miss my Mary, Cath, and Rich. One by one they have moved away to their own little Pads. These moves envolved those dreaded Suitcases with a lot more boxes, filling the car to the roof. This left a very small space for me to squeeze into. Off we would drive to the location, for me to check over the new premises. Once I had sniffed in all the corners and left the outside boundry mark scented, I felt happy that all was well for my young students.

I loved it best when my pack came back, as they aid at the time called Christmas.

First, and a most excellent sign, was a 'Fur Tree' planted in the Lounge. This tree was lit up with coloured lights which twinkled onto all sorts of shiny hangings. I liked to Lye on my rug and gaze at this sign, or sniff at the branches which sometimes smelt of doggy choc drops.

There was also a lot of cooky smells and especially pastry aroma. To prevent any scraps meeting the dust bin, this was a good time to stand in the kitchen doorway and keep the eye catching gaze fixed on those little pies. Secretly I would save the cook work by sneaking into the kitchen to vacuum up the crumbs from the floor. I think she appreciated this help.

Greeting my young people as they arrived home gave me the greatest joy. Once again our days were tied together. Sleeping in our accommodation with me between the two beds, At the lye-in I would rest thinking of our day ahead.

The festivities began as suit cases were carried in bringing The Grands, more food, and a lot of paper packages. Our clan sat around a real fire, we ate wonderful meaties with plenty of extra human food and bones for me. I would sit in the middle of wrapping papers having a stomach rub, with wafting food smells over my head, in the knowledge that we would be walking in the places I love best.

And so pastry time passed and I looked forward to the chocolate Egg time, Summer at the Grands, and visits to the little pads.

The years woofed by.

Learning

I am most proud of my pack and I am not boasting when I tell you that I have become the most learned of dogs. My young people were all students and they passed on to me knowledge. I have heard stories and listened to their homework. I have pondered over G.C.E. questions and sat on A Level papers. I have stayed at the Student Nurses Home and gained tips from the long haired Ham on R.G. N's.

I have visiting many Universities, leaving my mark in both Oxford and Cambridge.

I have stayed, at least for a day at The University of Sussex in Brighton, where I climbed the Downs; The Trent Poly, University status, Nottingham where I viewed the wide river Trent; and Chichester College, were I gain access to the car Park. I have walked around the Tower and garden of Imperial College London to understand how my Richard is to become a Doctor.

Mum instructed me, as we drove to her lecturers of in Nose to Nose Ventilation of the Life Saving technique, and I have been to see my Dad's officewhere I left a calling card by "Peeing on his Ponents".

Although I am being flippant or should I say pawpant, I do understand how important it is that my pack comprehend all aspects of this earths environment, and I hope that I have encouraged my pets in all their endeavours to become of service to all creatures great and small.

I said that I was a learned dog.

The Strolling Years

I had a new doggie walker in my older years. Her name is Bethan and she is the mistress of Mango. Bethan would call to take me out after school. Our evening routine started with my loud bark to make her jump, then she could attach my lead, and Mango and I trotted off to the bottom of the garden with this little mistress. Here Mango waved her tail to us and waited while Bethan and I strolled on around the marking circuit. On our return Mango would collect Bethan and take her home for tea.

I appreciated the treats, dog chews, which Bethan brought in for me because there was a lack of bones at home since Mum and Dad took smaller joints.

In these strolling years I was not able to see detail, but my scenting became markedly efficient. The Plumber came to renew our heating system and he laid out each new part on the floor for me to inspect. Using the long sniff method, I could tell that these 'ponents' had been stored in a good animal home and were suitable for our system, so it was ok for him to install into our house.

My runs these days took me into the Lane Paddock where the young wire hair would race over for a talk. Along the road I might pass the time of season with Candy the elderly Collie bitch, or nose gentle Captain through her back gate. Occasionally I would wander alone down our drive but before I reached the road mum would catch a me up and we would wander back to them gardens.

Most of all I liked to stand at the open my back door absorbing the wafting scenty in pictures which floated from our beautiful countryside and dream of the moment when Mary's car would race into the drive again.

A Dogs Day

I could never tire of listening to the voices of my dear pack, but every dog must have his day, and I have had 365 days x 16½ years. Every 6,022½ days have been filled with Dog Joy.

I am good at maths too!

There will never be another Rob Dog but there are plenty of my kindness. I will be my packs Guard-in-angle Dodge until another takes my responsibilities. Keeping you fit and leading your walkies, calming and guarding you, listening to troubles, wagging with joy and most important of all Always ready to welcome my pack home.

Then I am away with Gem and the rest into the Happy Hunting Ground where

"No dog barks up any wrong trees."